THE FRICK COLLECTION

Anshen Transdisciplinary Lectureships in Art, Science and the Philosophy of Culture

---

MONOGRAPH TWO

Previously Published:

MONOGRAPH ONE
THE REAL DISCOVERY OF AMERICA:
MEXICO, NOVEMBER 8, 1519
by
Hugh Thomas

THE ORIGIN OF THE UNIVERSE
AND THE ORIGIN OF RELIGION

by Sir Fred Hoyle

MOYER BELL

WAKEFIELD, RHODE ISLAND & LONDON

Published by Moyer Bell

First Edition

LIBRARY OF CONGRESS
CATALOGING-IN-PUBLICATION DATA

Hoyle, Fred, Sir.
    The origin of the universe and the
origin of religion / by Sir Fred Hoyle. —
1st ed.
        p.   cm. — (Anshen transdiscipli-
nary lectureships in art, science, and the
philosophy of culture ; monograph 2)
    1. Cosmology.   2. Religion—History.
3. Science—History. 4. Culture—
Origin.   5. Process philosophy.
I. Title.   II. Series.
QB985.H67   1993
523.1—dc20   92-26551
ISBN 1-55921-082-6   CIP

Printed in the United States of America

CONTENTS

INTRODUCTION

I am most happy, ladies and gentlemen, to welcome you to the second of the Anshen Transdisciplinary Lectureships in Art, Science and the Philosophy of Culture. Less than six months ago, in November of last year, we inaugurated this series with a lecture by Lord Thomas of Swynnerton concerning "the Real Discovery of America: Mexico, November 8, 1519." Tonight, we turn to other, much earlier realms of discovery, to origins in science and the universe, and to origins of culture and religion. It is again an honor and a deep pleasure to see so many remarkable scholars in our audience, distinguished persons representing all of the sciences and arts.

Our speaker this evening who will lead us into incredibly distant worlds—thirteen billion years ago—is a very celebrated, very controversial man who has all of his life thought for himself, and who has very frequently explored unknown, uncharted beginnings of galaxies and planets. Although knighted twenty years ago, and retired from his senior professorship in astronomy at Cambridge University at the same time, Sir Fred Hoyle remains more active than ever in the investigation of the organic composition of interstellar matter. His many new theories challenge old and new scholarship and research, and they remain as exciting and controversial as ever. His astonishing books concerning astronomy and astrophysics pour out as do novels and children's stories. Many of his books have become classic statements of this extraordinary pursuit of origins: *The Nature of the Universe, Frontiers of Astronomy, Man in the Universe, The Intelligent Universe*; we therefore eagerly await his present lecture.

After Sir Fred's speech, we shall have a discussion period, and a number of scholars have indicated an eagerness to participate in this. All of tonight's proceedings are being recorded, so may I please request that anyone contributing to the discussion use one of the microphones set up in the auditorium. We can also give you a portable microphone for your comments, should you prefer to use that. The discussion of it is led by Freeman Dyson, who has been Professor of Physics at the Institute for Advanced Study in Princeton since 1953. Like Sir Fred, Professor Dyson was born and educated in England, and spent his earliest university years at Cambridge, but Professor Dyson left Cambridge two years after his degree there to go to Cornell, and he has now lived more than forty years in the United States. Again like Sir Fred, he has written many popular scientific works as well as celebrated learned studies. Two of his best known, of course, are *Disturbing the Universe* and *Infinite in All Directions*. A list of the medals and honors and honorary degrees for both speakers, as you might expect, would fill many pages.

The entire program is under the direction of the founder of this series of lectures, Dr. Ruth Nanda Anshen. Dr. Anshen's philosophic mind is just as much at ease in inquiries concerning astrophysics and astronomy and the origins of the universe and of religion as it is with history and anthropology and the discovery of America. We salute her again this evening for her remarkable leadership and her own passionate pursuit of transdisciplinary studies. We salute her also for another remarkable book, just off the press—*Morals Equals Manners*; it has been greeted by those fortunate enough to read the text in galleys as a "passionate critique of our moral condition. . . . Ruth Nanda Anshen asks us to think again about essential matters we now ignore at our peril." It is her genius that has made this evening's program possible.

—Charles Ryskamp

PREFACE

This lecture by Sir Fred is an occasion prompting me to emphasize the importance of the philosophical and scientific actuality of *Process*. The principle of Process belongs to all disciplines and is therefore transdisciplinary. It also belongs to all life. It is a basic principle whose importance I learned a long time ago from my revered teacher, Alfred North Whitehead.

Process is synonymous with change and they cannot do without each other. It constitutes consciousness itself. The inaugural lecture in this hallowed place, The Frick Collection, was devoted to the process of history. This evening's lecture will be devoted to the process of the Universe and of Religion.

The constellations do not appear to change at all, but we know that they do. The process occurs in a minute or in two billion years. It is merely a matter of human measurement. We know that a piece of granite is a mass of activity, yet it is changing at a very slow rate, even though it appears to be permanent.

We gaze at the magnificent paintings here in this haven of culture, guarded by our inimitable and noble friend, Charles Ryskamp, and each time we are transfigured and enriched by a new experience of their beauty, meaning and superb art.

Our human bodies change from day to day. Their external appearance is the same, but their change is constant and sometimes visible. It is all a process. The process is itself the actuality whether we measure it by minutes or millennia. We ourselves are part of it.

Language also is a process moving from mythic cultures with their various symbolic systems ranging from cuneiform, hieroglyphic, ideographic to alphabetic and mathematical systems.

We have been brought into existence in a certain part of the Universe in consequence of its process and there is no reason to suppose that other types of existence, unimaginable to us, have not been produced elsewhere in the Universe. History itself is an example of process.

By history I refer not to the particular event such as, for example, that Brutus killed Caesar, but a process both more general and more primary. It constitutes the intercommunication between the inner being of actions and plans, and the inner being of the human self. History in this sense is the actual process of how the event took place.

Process is a form of energy, an effort to discover in things and bring out from things their own dynamic existence, their spirit conceived as a kind of invisible ghost which comes down to them from the spirit of the Universe and gives them their typical form of life and movement. Things themselves are not a dream, they have their own reality.

The process that has occurred within the past hundred years has changed not only the external conditions under which the average person, at least in the Western world, passes his life on earth. What we are dealing with are the dynamics of change in organisations, societies and communities. There is a process at work that begins with changes in perception, vision and leadership. A process that then continues as those changes lead to changes in culture, organisation and structure. And a process that finds its fulfillment as those changes in turn lead to changes in the actions of individuals, communities and societies. This process in a person's fundamental beliefs, in his conception of religion, in his whole world-outlook, is probably greater now than those that have occurred during the preceding four thousand years.

Life seems to remain static for thousands of years and then to shoot forward with amazing speed since the process was slowly being born within us as in society. The last century has been one of those periods of extraordinary changes, perhaps the most amazing in human history.

We stand at the brink of an age in which human life presses forward to actualize new forms. The unity of man and nature, of mind and matter, of time and space, of freedom and security, of subject and object, of process and change has given us a new vision of man in his organic unity and of history offering a richness and diversity of quality and majesty of scope hitherto unprecedented.

In relating the accumulated wisdom of our minds to the recognition that process is the actuality of life, these transdisciplinary lectures seek to encourage a renaissance of hope in society and of pride in our decision as to what our destiny will be. For the creative process in the human mind, the developmental process in organic nature and the basic laws of the inorganic realm may be but a varied expression of a universal formative process.

In spite of our infinite obligation and in spite of our finite power, in spite of the intransigence of nationalisms, and in spite of the conflicts of moral passions, beneath the turmoil and upheaval of the present, and out of the transformation of this dynamic period with the unfolding of a new world, these transdisciplinary lectures may help to quicken the "unshaken heart" of well-rounded truths and to actualize the significant elements now taking shape out of the core of that undimmed continuity of the creative process which favor the harmonious development of the senses, of the spirit, of the "vegetative soul" which man has in common with animals and plants and which restores man to mankind while deepening and enhancing his convergence with the universe.

—Ruth Nanda Anshen

THE ORIGIN OF THE UNIVERSE AND THE ORIGIN OF RELIGION

THE WAGES OF
RESPECTABILITY

Science is unique to human activities in that it possesses vast areas of certain knowledge. The collective opinion of scientists in these areas about any problem covered by them will almost always be correct. It is unlikely that much in these areas will be changed in the future, even in a thousand years. And because technology rests almost exclusively on these areas the products of technology work as they are intended to do.

But for areas of uncertain knowledge the story is very different. Indeed the story is pretty well the exact opposite, with the collective opinion of scientists almost always incorrect. There is an easy proof of this statement. Because of the large number of scientists nowadays and because of the large financial support which they enjoy, uncertain problems would mostly have been cleared up already if it were otherwise. So you can be pretty certain that wherever problems resist solution for an appreciable time by an appreciable number of scientists the ideas used for attacking them must be wrong. It is therefore a mistake to have anything to do with popular ideas for solving uncertain issues, and the more respectable the ideas may be the more certain it is that they are wrong.

There is a simple rule for avoiding being sucked into a maelstrom of respectable ignorance. Whenever the word 'origin' is used disbelieve everything you are told, even if it is I who am telling it. The biggest pig in a poke where origins are concerned is that of the whole universe. All the important action is supposed to have happened in the first fleeting moment, the stage being basically set in the first 10^{-43} seconds. Events it is supposed occurred from there until a time of about 10^{-23} seconds of a kind that physicists would dearly like to bring into the area of certain knowledge, but for which equipment to make relevant laboratory experiments is too costly, at any rate at present. After about 10^{-23} seconds the situation emerges into known territory, and after a time of a few seconds all effective physical action is over and done with. Thereafter the universe is supposed to expand apart as a huge explosion. Explosions do not usually lead to a well-ordered situation. An explosion in a junk yard does not lead to sundry bits of metal being assembled into useful working machines. Yet after expanding for about a billion years something of this nature is supposed to have happened to the universe. Galaxies formed that are widely similar over large volumes of space. Stars formed. Life originated and evolved. Man arose and began to think about it all. How such a structured world came into being remains unexplained. Not for want of effort, however. For a quarter of century or more cosmologists have tried to relate what is supposed to have happened in the first fleeting second to the ordered world which developed several billions of years later—so far with more sound and fury than success, and in the absence of clear and unequivocal success in relating events in the first seconds to what happened later, the position lacks causality. All that we see in the universe of observation and fact, as opposed to the mental state of scenario and supposition, remains unexplained. And even in its supposedly first second the universe is itself acausal. That is to say, the universe has to know in advance what it is going to be before it knows how to start itself. For in accordance with the Big Bang Theory for instance, at a time of 10^{-43} seconds the universe has to know how many types of neutrino there are going to be at a time of 1 second. This is so in order that it starts off expanding at the right rate to fit the eventual number of neutrino types. This is by no means the only acausal property the universe apparently has to be aware of before it begins. In the fourth of his Pegram Lectures, given at the Brookhaven National Laboratory in 1989, Denys Wilkinson drew up an extended list of properties where the universe seemingly has to know what it is going to do before it does them. The list is extensive enough to make a cynic out of any reasonable person. Or as the older folk would have said it in my youth, enough to make a cat laugh.

Another big one for the book is the origin of life, which according to respectable opinion happened here on the Earth. Imagine the Earth's history to be represented by a single day. Then the origin of life did not occur in the last 20 hours because there is fossil evidence that life has existed over the last 20 hours. Nor did life originate in the first 3½ hours, because in this early period the Earth was so heavily bombarded by missiles from outside that even rocks were pulverized so violently as to be unable to preserve their integrity. So life, if it originated on the Earth, did so between 03:30 a.m. and 04:00 a.m. We therefore ask for the evidence that the amazing biochemical miracle of the origin of life happened in this comparatively brief window in the Earth's history. A few sedimentary rocks have survived from it, but they have unfortunately been heated so much that any fossil evidence of life and its origin which might have existed have been lost. Thus the evidence for the respectable popular belief is nil. This is one remarkable aspect of the popular belief, that it is founded on nothing. The other remarkable aspect is the intensity of the opprobrium one incurs if one denies it. Only a little biochemical knowledge is needed to see this is yet another situation to set the cats in an uproar.

Biology is replete with them. We are told that natural selection acts to spread small advantageous mutations and operates to suppress disadvantageous ones. But small changes must be frequent if a species is to go anywhere much, in which case the bad and the good are superposed on each other, and how then does natural selection manage to separate them? With the bad generally accepted to be more frequent than the good, all natural selection can do, in simple replicative systems at any rate, is to minimise the rate at which things get worse.

You would think this problem would have been addressed with some care, but as far as I can see it never is. The fossil record of the last 500 millions years provides a serious indictment of biological thinking on evolution. It provides ample evidence of small changes and little or none of big changes. So if evolution is correct, as I suspect it to be, the big changes occur swiftly and the small changes slowly, the big changes so swiftly that they cannot be captured by the random moments revealed by the fossil record. As a physicist might put it, evolution takes place through a sequence of delta-functions, not smoothly as according to respectable scientific academies it is supposed to do.

More than a century ago Alfred Russel Wallace noticed that the higher qualities of Man are acausal, like the Universe itself. Where human qualities have been honed by evolution and natural selection there is very little difference between one individual and another. Given equivalent opportunities for training, healthy human males of age 20 will hardly differ in their abilities to run at pace by more than 10 percent between the Olympic runner and the average. But for the higher qualities it is very much otherwise. From enquiries among teachers of art, Wallace estimated that for every child who draws instinctively and correctly there are a hundred that don't. The proportions are much the same in music and mathematics. And for those who are outstanding in these fields the proportions are more like one in a million. Having made this point Wallace then made the striking argument that, while the abilities with small spread like running would have been important to the survival of primitive man, the higher qualities had no survival value at all. Over a span of 12 years spent in the Amazon and in the forests of the East Indies, Wallace is said to have discovered 30,000 new species off his own bat. He lived by shipping his specimens to an agent in London who then marketed them to museums. During most of the time, when he wasn't writing epoch-making papers on biological evolution, he lived with primitive tribesmen. Wallace therefore knew a great deal about the modes of survival of primitive man, probably more than anybody else of his generation and probably more than anybody does today. His views on the matter therefore carry weight. What he said was that in his experience he never saw a situation in which an aptitude for mathematics would have been of help to primitive tribes. So little numerate were they that in 12 years he saw only a few who could count as far as 10. His conclusion was the higher qualities, the qualities with large variability from individual to individual, had not been derived from natural selection. Abilities derived from natural selection have small spread. Abilities not derived from natural selection have wide spreads.

Wallace was writing only a decade after Maxwell's work on electromagnetic fields, which even in physics were still seen as mysterious. It therefore seemed reasonable to speculate that perhaps there was some universal field which acted on matter so as to produce intelligence once evolution had advanced to a suitable stage. This is an idea which still resurfaces from time to time. But today it comes so close to offending areas of certain knowledge that for me, at any rate, it has no plausibility. I think the higher qualities must be of genetic origin, the same as the rest. The mystery is that we have to be endowed with the relevant genes in advance of them being useful. The time order of events is inverted from what we would normally expect it to be, a concept that is of course gall and wormwood to respectable opinion. The objection is that it explodes one's concepts, raising all manner of new ideas. Which is exactly what respectability dislikes, because it is only in times of stagnation that respectability flourishes.

In recent years I have managed to earn the dislike of respectable societies by saying that natural history was nearer to the truth in the first half of the 19th century than in the second half. Already in 1813, in a lecture to the Royal Society of London, William Wells described the process of evolution by natural selection. In the early 1830's it was being asked how this process might go in detail. Could it explain evolution on a large scale, as in the well-known picture of evolution occurring like a branching tree? General opinion was that it could not, and for a reason that was good and which was never answered in the enthusiasms of the later Darwinian movement. It was observed that plants and animals always, or almost always, have limited habitats, usually with quite sharp boundaries in which they thrive and outside which they do not. Why, if evolution could produce very large differences like those between horses, bears and primates, could it not produce the much smaller differences that would serve to enable species to extend their limited habitants? Why did each species not have the plasticity (as it was called) to spread itself all over the world? The fact that this emphatically was not what happened suggested that, while by selection each species fine-tuned its abilities within the range accessible to it, the range in every case is small, far smaller than would be needed to produce the difference between horses and bears.

ICE AGES AND COMETS

My introduction now over, let me move closer to the main topic of my lecture, beginning with the ice-ages of the last million years, which are widely accepted as having had an important influence on human development.

Thirteen thousand years ago, New York was covered by several hundred metres of ice, as it had been for most of the preceding hundred thousand years. Then with startling suddenness the glaciers over Scandinavia and N. America disappeared. In Britain the temperature shot up from a summertime value of only 8°C to 18°C, and it did so in a few decades, in a flash from an historic point of view. How do we know this? From beetles. If I have been somewhat derisory to this point let me redress the balance a little. By speaking up for beetles, British beetles especially. Diverse species of beetles prosper at different temperatures in a sensitive way. There are species that can exist at 10°C which cannot at 8°C, others which can exist at 12°C which cannot at 10°C, and so on. Layers of mud which formed annually on the bottoms of unfrozen lakes in the south of England give a calendar of events which can be counted year by year. So by painstakingly searching through the layers of mud looking for beetle remains, especially with regard to the temperature sensitivities of the beetle species you have accurate summer temperatures as they were in Britain 13,000 years ago, an excellent fossilised thermometer. I count it as one of the redeeming features of the human species that it produces individuals who are prepared to spend their whole lives searching through layers of mud for beetles in order to acquire this kind of knowledge.

A similar event occurred about 40,000 years ago. There was a similar sudden warming and a similar quick melting of glaciers in N. Europe. It was then that *Homo Sapiens* appeared in Europe, then that the wonderful art of cave painting seems to have begun. But warmer times did not last on that earlier occasion. After the initial warm pulse there was a steady deterioration over a few thousand years back again into full blown ice-age conditions. Just the same deterioration happened following the warm pulse of 13,000 years ago. By 10,000 years ago the glaciers were back again but not yet to their full extent. In N. Britain they covered the mountain tops but did not extend down into the valley bottoms. It was then that the spectacular and beautiful upper mountain scenery, what in Scotland are called the upper corries, were carved by ice—I daresay that in the mountains of New Hampshire it is the same. Then 10,000 years ago there occurred a second warm pulse. Once again within a human lifetime the temperature shot up spectacularly by 10 degrees Celsius, all in a moment from an historic point of view. And this second pulse did the trick. It brought the Earth's climate out of the ice-age of the last hundred thousand years into a warm interglacial period which has been essential for the development of history and civilisation. The position is indeed quite like the way it is with history, where we know a great deal of the factual side of what happened but comparatively little of the reasons why.

The reason why there have been ice-ages has been infuriatingly difficult to discover. During ice-ages tropical mountains like Mauna Kea in Hawaii carried glaciers which quite rules out recently popular theories of an astronomical nature, which do not change the supply of sunlight to the Earth as a whole, whereas ice on tropical mountains shows that the entire Earth was cooled, and indeed cooled very appreciably. If one keeps the reflectivity of the Earth fixed and makes a greenhouse calculation with an appreciably reduced amount of water vapour in the atmosphere the result is just like the way it was in an ice-age. Dry conditions with a fall of 10 degrees Celsius in the average temperature of the whole Earth, dry conditions with glaciers accumulating slowly but inexorably, millimetre by millimetre, and with cool oceans giving low evaporation rates responsible for the reduced water vapour in the atmosphere. This is a self-consistent explanation subject to the Earth reflecting as much sunlight back into space as it does at present. It is here that the problem arises, however, for with significantly less water in the atmosphere one would expect less cloud and less reflection back into space, when the penetration of more sunlight to ground-level would produce a compensating warming effect. Thus to save the explanation some other source of reflection is needed, as for instance a haze in the upper atmosphere such as is known to be produced by large volcanic explosions. The explosion of Mt. Tambora in the E. Indies in 1815 led to the failure of crops in New England in 1816, due to a cooling caused by the resulting haze of small particles in the high atmosphere. An even more drastic effort occurred in AD 536 when the haze from a volcanic explosion in the previous year led to a failure of the vine crop in the Mediterranean, the haze being so strong that except for an hour or two around midday the disk of the Sun was fogged-out even on otherwise clear days.

The problem with this explanation is that volcanic haze in modern times has not persisted for more than a few years, because it soon gets washed out by the water in the atmosphere. Perhaps under much dryer conditions volcanic haze persists for much longer. Another possibility is that tiny crystals of ice form, in which case even small quantities of water could provide an effective haze. Very low temperatures are needed to produce such crystals; below -50°C, and fortunately except in rare conditions in arctic regions such conditions do not occur today. But perhaps they did during the ice-age. At all events what seems to be needed to produce an ice-age is the combination of a dry atmosphere with high-level haze.

My main concern here, however, is not so much with the genesis of an ice-age as with its ending. What all in a

moment can destroy a situation with a longevity running
into tens of thousands of years? Evidently only an exceedingly catastrophic event of some kind, something that
would wash-out high-level haze, increasing the water-
vapour greenhouse sufficiently to send the temperature
up almost instantaneously by the 10 degrees Celsius
clearly registered in the beetle record. But more still, for
unless there was also a change from a cold ocean to a
warm ocean the situation would soon return to where it
was before. The difference between a warm ocean and a
cold one amounts to about a 10-year supply of sunlight.
Thus the warm conditions produced by a strong water-
vapour greenhouse must be maintained for at least a
decade in order to produce the required transformation of
the ocean, and this is just about the time for which water,
suddenly thrown up into the stratosphere, might be
expected to persist there. The needed amount of water is
so vast, 100 million million tons, that only one kind of
causative event appears possible, the infall of a comet-
sized object into a major ocean. A volcanic event falls
short of what is needed by a huge margin.

We know for certain that many such comet-sized impacts have occurred over geologic periods. Where impacts occur on the land surface detectable craters are
formed and rocks are fused and evaporated to form the
small glass buttons known as tektites, of which myriads
have been scattered widely from points of impact. The
surprise is that a violent form of event, to which the
time-scale of occurrence has been set at millions of years,
should have happened as recently as 13,000 years ago
and again for a second time at 10,000 years ago. This

would clearly not be possible unless something unusual has happened to the environs of the Earth over the past 15,000 years. What has been unusual, according to Victor Clube and Bill Napier, has been the arrival in a periodic Earth-crossing orbit of a giant comet, a comet a thousand to ten-thousand times more massive than an average comet like Halley's. By 'Earth-crossing' is meant an orbit which at its closest to the Sun is less than the radius of the Earth's orbit, a necessary condition for a comet, or more likely a fragment of a comet, to hit the Earth. By a 'periodic' comet is meant one whose largest distance from the Sun does not exceed by any large margin the radii of the orbits of the outermost planets, which means that periodic comets revolve around their orbit in times ranging from a few years to a few thousand years.

Comets normally move in orbits of much greater size, never coming into the regions of the planets. Normal comet orbits of great size are occasionally changed to the much smaller orbit of a periodic comet by a combination of two unusual occurrences. The first is the passage of the solar system as a whole in its motion in the Galaxy close to some massive aggregate, as for instance to a molecular cloud. This inevitably puts a small fraction of the many comets which inhabit the outermost distant regions of the solar system into orbits that are exceedingly elongated, with closest distances from the Sun that cross the orbits of the outer planets. Then the gravitational influence of the outer planet in question changes the orbit again, greatly reducing its elongation so that it no longer recedes back to the most distant regions from which it came. By the combination of these two gravitational effects comets are captured into the region of the planets. Although unusual and improbable there are so many comets that it happens for some of them, as it has done for Comet Halley. What Clube and Napier propose is that some 15,000 years ago the process happened for a comet that was also unusual in being far more massive than Halley's, thus adding a third exceptional circumstance to the other two.

My first impression on encountering this proposal was that a third exceptional circumstance was one too many. I could agree that among the hundreds of billions of comets which are thought to exist in the most distant regions some will be more massive than others, and occasionally there will be one far more massive than others, perhaps one in ten thousand of the kind that Clube and Napier call a giant comet. Such a monster might be expected to become a periodic comet, not every few thousand years but every few tens of millions of years. Why then the coincidence that it seems to have happened as recently as 15,000 years ago? Then I saw that the answer to this question lies in what nowadays is called the anthropic principle, which says that the fact of our existence can be used to discount all improbabilities necessary for our existence. If history and civilisation were caused by the arrival of a periodic giant comet all accident is removed from our association in time with such a comet. The arrival of the comet was random but our association with the effects of the comet is not. This then is the assertion: The whole of history and civilisation has been caused by the arrival of a periodic giant comet in an Earth-crossing orbit some 15,000 years ago.

To get to grips with this matter we must therefore study in a little detail what a comet really is.

What a comet is not is a dirty snowball, the supposedly respectable theory contradicted by every aspect of the approach to the Earth in 1986 of Comet Halley and by events since then. No dirty snowball at a temperature of -200°C ever exploded as Comet Halley did in March 1991. Dirty snowballs are not blacker than jet black. On March 30–31, 1986, Comet Halley ejected a million tons of fine particles which on being warmed by the Sun emitted radiation characterised by organic materials, not dirt as one understands dirt. When heated sufficiently a snowball would evaporate smoothly, whereas Comet Halley evaporated in a sequence of explosions that continued as the Comet receded from the Sun long after ordinary evaporation would have ceased. Nothing in the behaviour of Comet Halley has been like that of any normal object of which we are familiar.

It is possible that comets in their early days contained enough radioactive materials delivering sufficient heat for them to become melted. Then after the radioactivity died away and heat ceased to be released internally within them freezing would take place. Since water was a common constituent, consider how a liquid sphere with a radius of ten to a hundred kilometres in a distant region from the Sun would freeze. Not as a solid sphere of ice. Freezing would occur from the outside inwards. Once a frozen outer shell had formed there would be insufficient room for liquid water inside the shell to go solid, for the reason that water expands on freezing, as every householder who has experienced burst water pipes in winter knows. The surface shell would be cracked open and liquid still in the interior would spurt outwards through the cracks, freezing itself as it did so. Only by repeated cracking and by liquid making room for itself on the outside could such a body go eventually solid, with the ice everywhere stressed by the freezing at pressures of about 30 atmospheres. Now add other liquids with lower freezing points than water, as have many organic liquids, some hydrocarbons for example. These would be especially subject to spurting outwards through the multitude of cracks that would thread the entire bulk of the comet, causing the most volatile materials to be forced to the outer surface, or ejected away entirely into space.

Consider such an object becoming gravitationally deflected into an Earth-crossing orbit and so becoming heated even more fiercely than the terrestrial tropics at its closest approach to the Sun. In the early revolutions around such an orbit there would be a huge evaporation of highly volatile materials from the comet, followed by a gradual dissolution of the many pieces into which the original body became divided by the cracking process. As the jointings of the pieces became progressively weakened by repeated heatings, the division would happen under pressures of some 30 atmospheres, essentially suddenly as the jointings lost strength. A pressure of 30 atmospheres is about 450 pounds per square inch, capable when released of making quite a fizz, for a body of cometary size effectively an explosion. The reason why Comet Halley was able to undergo a major dissolutary event, even though it had receded in March 1991 beyond the orbit of Saturn towards that of Uranus, a distance of some 2 billion kilometres from the Sun, was that the jointings of its pieces had been weakened by the approach of 1986 and as with the breaking of solid structures the thing went suddenly, releasing internal pressures like a mass of coiled springs.

Thus after an initial rush of evaporated highly volatile materials, the process is dominated by subdivision into many pieces, each piece evaporating more slowly over hundreds of revolutions of the orbit as the pieces become coated at their surfaces by cooked organic material, which may conveniently be thought of as black tar. This was exactly as Comet Halley appeared visually in 1986, as a body coated by black tar, not a dirty snowball, unless by 'dirt' one means tar.

Return now to the question of cometary chunks hitting the Earth. The chance of collision at each orbital revolution of the original undivided comet is small, only about one part in a billion. Thus in 10,000 years there would only at most be a chance of a few parts in a million of the undivided comet colliding with the Earth. But as the comet divides into more and more and more chunks the chance of one or another of them hitting the Earth rises inexorably, until one or another of them will indeed score a bullseye on our planet. This will happen over a 10,000 year interval when the original comet has divided into about a million pieces. For such a collision to be capable of ending an ice age the colliding piece must have been pretty large, say 10,000 million tons, and if this was only a millionth of the original comet then the comet at first must have had a mass of 10,000 million million tons, which is just what Clube and Napier call a giant comet.

Terrible deductions follow. As the pieces become smaller and smaller, collisions become more and more frequent, until with the pieces down to a million tons apiece, corresponding to a size of about 100 metres, there would be an impact rate of about one per year. An event of this kind actually happened in the early hours of 1 July 1908. The atmospheric flash of light was so great as to be seen by a Miss K. Stephen of Godmanchester, Huntingdonshire at shortly after midnight on 1 July. It was not until 1927, however, that an expedition penetrated to the region of the Tunguska river in Siberia, to discover a scene of peculiar devastation. Instead of impacting the ground the incoming body broke into fragments at a height in the atmosphere probably of about 10 kilometres. The immense blast wave had felled trees to a distance of scores of kilometres, or had burned them on account of the great heat released. The resulting roar must have been like ten thousand thunderclaps rolled into one. Human survival must have been problematical over an area of some thousands of square miles.

Such events, occurring at an average rate for the whole Earth of about 1 per year, clear up a puzzling problem from immediate prehistory, the problem of the discovery of metal smelting. The possibility of obtaining bright metal from a piece of stone could hardly have occurred to anyone as an abstract concept, so impossible would it appear until after the discovery had actually been made. Thus the discovery must surely have been made by accident. The problem has hitherto been to understand how the same remarkable accident could have occurred independently in all the widely-separated places where archaeological evidence shows that copper was being used in the production of tools at dates before about 4000 BC. To avoid the need for independent discoveries archaeologists were led *circa* 1950 to what became known as the diffusion theory, according to which the discovery was made at one location only, and was carried from there to other places, implying a greater mobility of peoples than had previously been expected. After some two decades of popularity the diffusion theory ran into the difficulty that other artefacts which might also have been spread with copper smelting were not widely diffused in the same way. Now we have the answer to independent accidents, however, thereby clearing up a major prehistoric conundrum.

In places where there were forests, events of the Tunguska kind must have started immense fires, producing masses of glowing charcoal. Where veins of metallic ores came up from below to the ground surface, smelting would take place naturally. Thereafter nomadic tribes could have come on the smelted copper in diverse places and simply picked it up. The smelting would not be very pure, which is probably why copper was the first metal to appear in archaeological records. Iron with a few percent of impurities is brittle and useless stuff. Copper, on the other hand, even impure copper, is hard enough and malleable enough to be immediately useful to people accustomed only to stone implements. The copper could be beaten into a multitude of shapes, yielding tools of all kinds and eventually weapons—daggers, swords, arrow heads, spears and shields.

Table: Events Fitted to an Impact Period of 1600 Years

Dates	Event
BC	
10,700	Strike of major bolide ends ice age
9,100	Lesser impacts produce extinction of woolly mammoth
7,500	Second large bolide strike confirms end of ice-age
5,900	Metals smelted naturally
4,300	Metals smelted naturally. Beginning of Homeric religions
2,700	End of Egyptian Old Dynasty Pyramid construction starts shortly thereafter
1,100	Origin of Judaism. Joshua
AD	
500	Decline of Roman Empire. Origin of Islam
2,100	Next strike, probably with reduced intensity

THE GENERAL
SITUATION IN
POST-ICE AGE TIMES

Much that is true in the millennia B.C. follows from these considerations. On the basis that the comet in question has a period of 1600 years and that one of its nodal distances is the same as the Earth's distance from the Sun, with a shallow angle between the planes of the comet's orbit and the Earth's, the chance of a piece of it hitting the Earth is considerably higher than for a random situation, about 1 in 10 million rather than 1 in 1000 million. Division into pieces with sizes of about a kilometre would give an average of about 1 strike per passage. Division into pieces of diameter 100 metres would give 1000 strikes like Tunguska at each passage. Because the pieces tend to spread along the comet's orbit a passage through the inner solar system would last for the entire chain of pieces perhaps for several decades or even a century, giving an average strike rare for Tunguska-type events of about 10 per year. The consequences of such episodic bombardments, spaced by 1600 years, are given in the preceding table.

Whole herds of mammoths perished all in a moment. They did so by a sudden melting of the permafrost on which they spent their lives, causing them to become immersed in icy water, which then refroze within a matter of hours. Only a blast of heat from the sky could have had such an effect, a blast such as occurred at the Tunguska river.

Turning again to metal smelting, because nomads occupied the forest areas of post ice-age times the discoverers had to be wandering peoples who chanced on the naturally-smelted metal, in diverse places without any reference to each other. We also see why sedentary people, those in Mediterranean regions and the Near East, living by early agriculture in the river valleys, were hardly ever a match in war for barbarian invaders with metal weapons from the north. We also see what it was that rained down fire on the cities of Sodom and Gommorah, and it had nothing to do with what later preachers claimed it had. We can also have a pretty good idea of what it was that Joshua saw in the sky, not the Sun standing still but the distant glow of an immense fireball. The city of Jericho lies on a major earthquake line, so that the fall of the walls of Jericho can readily be attributed to a major earthquake. It is also true that lights in the sky are often associated with large earthquakes. But one might think it unlikely that such lights could have been intense enough for them to have been represented as a major miracle. The biblical account seems more like the experience of Miss K. Stephen of Godmanchester, except seen from a much closer distance. Miss Stephen had been two thousand miles or more away from the fireball of 1908, Joshua might only have been fifty miles.

Viewed in this way the writer of the biblical story can be seen to have done very well. He has got the two essential features, the bright light in the sky and the shattering of the city. But to make the story appear comprehensible he has added the mythical touches of the Sun hovering in the sky and the fall of the city to the sound of trumpets. The story then created havoc, when in later millennia the mythical touches were made to appear the reality rather than the original events which gave rise to them. On hearing of the heliocentric theory of Copernicus, Martin Luther remarked: "The fool would overturn all of astronomy. In the Holy Scriptures we read that Joshua ordained the Sun to stand still, not the Earth." Starting from a widely-held belief, the inviolable truth of the Scriptures, Luther thus destroyed Copernicus in a single perceptive stroke. Except of course it was the widely-held respectable belief, which Luther could not bring himself to question, that was wrong, not Copernicus. This should be a frightening example to many modern scientists who argue just as Luther did, by impeccable logic from a false starting point. When a starting point is wrong the more impeccable the logical development the worse the result. A man of modest means who believes he is a millionaire will find that the more consistently he behaves in accordance with his hypothesis the worse his case becomes. The only defence against wrong hypotheses is poor logic, curiously enough.

If I may insert a little personal history, I had a moment of sudden insight on all this in my early teens. I was brought up in a small village in which the local church played a dominating social role, making it unthinkable for me to have stayed out of it. At the grammar school in a nearby town, which by then I attended, we had classes in religious instruction. The situation was quite unlike the American scene where such a situation would be anathema. But the situation never did me any harm. Indeed quite the reverse, for I always found that in examinations on religious instruction it was easy to pick up high marks. This was Church of England. What of Catholics you might ask? Well, Catholics went to Catholic schools. Whether that did them any harm I can't say. And Jews went to Jewish schools. Whether that did them any harm I can't say because I never went to a Jewish school either.

Anyway, by the time I reached my early teens I had heard a powerful lot of sermons, ranging from wildly ranting lay preachers up to no less a person than William Temple, then Archbishop of York. Inevitably therefore I had come on many contradictions. Not just the Christian miracles that continue to torment modern commentators in the Anglican Church, but contradictions of behaviour and psychology, at any rate as it seemed to me. And just as I puzzled about problems in science and mathematics, so I puzzled about these seeming contradictions in religion. I think it was important that in my puzzlement I set a logical contradiction as having a higher status than a belief. Children perceive contradictions long before they become exposed to social beliefs. Unless they continue to permit contradictions to override later beliefs then I suspect brain damage will be the result. Once the brain is forced into accepting contradictions, ignoring them, turning a blind eye, it goes quickly into Christmas pudding.

What I tried at first in attempting to resolve religious contradictions was to find a minimum set of beliefs that would be free from contradiction, pretty well what modern 'advanced' Anglicans try to do. I had gone along in this fashion for more than a year when I suddenly saw, all in a moment, that the minimum set had to be null. There was not a single belief that I could accept as true without accurate argument not leading to contradiction, not anything of appreciable moment anywhere in Luther's 'Holy Scriptures' that I could take on trust, and nothing in any other religion. With this realisation all the problems were instantly gone. Unlike some who go through far greater agony of mind to make this step, I did not turn positive into negative, belief into disbelief. Statements in the Bible could be true or untrue as the case might be. Without extraneous evidence one did not know which. The essential point was that nothing was solid enough to form a basis for arguing about the nature of the physical world. Belief in a mix of myth and fact can lead only too easily, as the example of Martin Luther shows, to grotesquely wrong conclusions. On the other hand, a mixture of myth and fact can be very interesting if it is approached, as in the case of Joshua's trumpets, from another direction.

The grammar school I attended was small—I doubt we ever had as many as ten 'masters' as they were called. They all doubled in subjects other than their own. In particular, the classics master was also the history master.

It happened after I had specialised in science and mathematics that he was in administrative charge of my form
over a period of three years, during which we had many
impromptu conversations, some on historical matters. It
was from Edward E. Dodd, a diminutive fiery Welshman
who drove his small car around the countryside at a
lethal speed, that I came to accept that every surviving
historical document or story very probably has an element of truth in it. Otherwise the story would not have
survived. When an historic account has unbelievable
aspects to it, like the standstill of the Sun in Joshua, it
doesn't mean the story is wrong. It means the story hasn't
been told in the right context. With this realisation I have
kept a watch over the years for historical situations which
clearly do not make sense the way they are usually told,
the intriguing question being to discover what surprising
circumstance it was that really lay behind them. There is
an interesting example in Volume I of Winston
Churchill's *History of the English Speaking Peoples*. Of
the famous battle of AD 937 between Vikings and Saxons,
Churchill wrote:

> "(At Brunnenburgh in Northumberland) . . . the
> whole of N. Britain—Celtic, Danish, and Norwegian,
> pagan and Christian—together presented a hostile front
> (against the Saxon army) under Constantine, King of
> Scots, and Olaf of Dublin, with Viking reinforcements from
> Norway . . . The armies, very large for those impover-
> ished times, took up their stations as if for the Olympic
> Games, and much parleying accompanied the process.
> Tempers rose high as these masses of manhood flaunted
> their shields and blades at one another and flung gibes
> across a narrow space; and there was presently a fierce

clash between the Northumbrian and Icelandic Vikings and a part of the English army . . . the English were worsted. But on the following day the real trial of strength was staged. The rival hosts paraded in all the pomp of war, and then in hearty goodwill fell on with spear, axe and sword . . . The victory of the English was overwhelming . . ."

For the previous 150 years or more the Vikings had hardly lost a skirmish or a battle to the Saxons. So one can begin by wondering how they came to lose so decisively in AD 937, despite mustering support from so many quarters—Ireland, Iceland, N. Britain, Denmark and Norway. Did men really come from so far merely to flaunt their manhood and fling gibes at the Saxons? Or was there some compelling reason? And the Celts and Vikings were long-term enemies. So what impelled the Celts now to fight alongside their enemies? Without answers to these questions Churchill's account surely lacks credibility.

Without knowledge of the contents of ice-cores taken from glaciers in Greenland, anyone seeking to interpret the situation at Brunnenburgh would be likely to be led into fiction rather than history. Measurements of the acid content of year-by-year depositions of ice give an index of volcanic activity. The largest signal of the millennium, larger than that of 1816 for Mt. Tambora, occurred in AD 935. The resulting atmospheric haze in northern latitudes must have been like the situation in AD 536 when the disk of the Sun could not be seen except for an hour or two around midday, and then only as a pallid disk in the sky. Crops must have failed in northern latitudes just as they did in New England in 1816. Probably the volcano in question was in Iceland, in which case its worst effects would be felt in the far north, permitting the Saxons to do better on their richer farms in the south of England. So the Vikings came together because they were starving, likely enough in 937 with the crops failing for the second year in succession. They came together to acquire food from the Saxons. The Celts fought with them because they too were starving. Nor did it make any difference whether the Vikings were pagan or Christian. The parlay was not to fling insults or to flaunt anything. The parlay was for food. Because the Saxons refused it the battle was fought, and because the Vikings were more weakened by starvation they lost it. Such is undoubtedly the correct explanation, far from the bright martial colours in which Churchill paints his account. It was a sad situation not an heroic one. The heroics were supplied by later Saxon writers who created the myth that Churchill followed. I have to suspect that much of what we call history has been painted over in a similar way.

COMETS AND THE
ORIGIN OF RELIGIONS

So let us return to the problem of the disintegration of comets, and in particular to the dissolution of the giant comet of Clube and Napier. With dissolution into a million or more pieces we can understand the major events which terminated the last ice-age.* Further subdivision into a billion pieces each with a diameter of the order of 100 metres produced a situation in which the Earth was hit by a Tunguska-like impact about once each year on a long-term average and at bunched rates of 10 to 100 per year during the passage of the giant cometary swarm through the inner regions of the solar system, a situation which permits us to understand the remarkable

---

*A kilometer sized object falling into a major ocean would throw up a vast quantity of water into the atmosphere, leading to fantastically heavy rainfall. My friend Donald D. Clayton asks if this would be the real origin of the story of Noah.

discovery of metal smelting, a discovery which could hardly have been anticipated intellectually. Now let us bring in a further dramatic physical effect.

Clube and Napier attribute the rises and falls of civilisations to these bunchings of Tunguska-like events, falls during the shorter bad periods of intense impacts and rises over the longer much more extended free intervals. The bad periods generated religions, harsh and dark of hue, while in the longer free intervals the previous strong and sombre beliefs became smoothed and more light-hearted. Clube and Napier consider the dissolution of their giant comet to have been at its maximum some six or seven thousand years ago, when evaporation of volatile material must have produced spectacular displays in the night sky, with scores and perhaps even thousands of normal comet-sized bodies spewing out jets of gas and small particles in the manner of the tails of comets. It was this brilliant display in the night sky, accompanied by impacts on to the Earth, that led to the belief in ancient cultures of a war of the gods, with the impacts seen as misdirected shots in that war. As the evaporation eventually died away the war came to an end. Surely there would be one last highly visible object that would continue firing out its jets after the others had ceased. In legend this last object became Zeus, King of the Gods, who with his bolts had at last overwhelmed the others.

Metal smelting, the demise of the mammoths, and the bolts of Zeus are perhaps the strongest circumstantial reasons for believing in these ideas, although the pyramids of Egypt might be considered to run these three close, as we will see in a moment. The oldest description of beliefs from about 6000 years ago, known to me, is in *Genesis* and in the stories of Homer, both written early in the first millennium B.C., both written some thousands of years—perhaps 4000 years—after the events they seek to describe, and both doubtless considerably distorted from the way things really were. Of the two, I consider Homer to have been less influenced by strong beliefs of relatively recent origin, and so it is to Homer that I would give main attention in this regard.

The overriding feature of both the *Iliad* and the *Odyssey*, it seems to me, is the absence of human will as a causative agent. Although the causative agent controlling humans has become brightly painted into the forms of gods and goddesses, there is still no doubt as to the direction from which the agent acts, from above, from the sky. Homer's stories, delivered orally, would hardly have carried conviction with his audiences unless a belief in the sky as an ever-present danger had persisted in popular belief from earlier times. But with inevitable distortions induced by long intervals of freedom from the danger. One such distortion was the replacement of missile impact by flashes of lightning. After many generations free from missile impact, a flash of lightning followed by rolling thunder was presumably the best description that could be given to the bolts of Zeus. But like Churchill's flaunting of weapons at Brunnenburgh, it doesn't ring true as soon as one thinks a little about it.

Very few people are killed by lightning and none by thunder, impressive as thunder may sound. But many people were drowned in Greek times in storms at sea. The *Odyssey* is indeed based on the difficulties in Homer's time of sea voyages in the Mediterranean. According to Homer, disasters at sea were caused either by the whims or the anger of the god Poseidon. Yet in the Greek pantheon Poseidon was inferior to Zeus, which would be to judge him who commanded a real and ever-present danger inferior to another who only commanded a largely illusory danger. But make the bolts of Zeus into Tunguska-like events and the situation becomes very different. This argument alone seems almost sufficient to prove the correctness of the Clube-Napier picture.

Ancient Egypt was the one culture that came within sighting distance of connecting the events of prehistory with the clear light of written history. And ancient Egypt had buildings that have survived for almost 5000 years, and so have gone through at least one severe period of impacts of a Tunguska-like character. This raises the question of what kind of a building would be best suited to surviving the blast wave from a cometary object 100 metres in diameter disintegrating at a height of 5 to 10 kilometres above it? I can think of nothing better than a pyramid.

In bad periods no human leader could stand against the power of natural events from the sky, which led to the concept of a god or gods transcending human authority. In lengthy good intervals, on the other hand, there was nothing except disease and death to challenge the power of absolute rulers. Nothing happened in the sky as religion claimed it could. Thus divinities tended to be downgraded, mostly by replacing an especially powerful god by a pantheon to which absolute rulers were ambitious to belong. So it certainly was with the Egyptian

Pharaohs. To join the pantheon after death it was necessary to be buried above ground and to be so in a manner
strong enough to stand against an assault from the sky. If
this be granted as the motive, there hardly seems any
better way of satisfying it than by building an impressive
pyramid, solid throughout except for a single entrance
passage to the royal burial chamber. It would be an
interesting experiment to see if a pyramid would survive
the blast from an impacting cometary object 100 metres in
diameter, disintegrating in the atmosphere above it at an
altitude of 5 to 10 kilometres. My impression is that it
would, and my impression is also that no other human
building could succeed in doing so. Without this explanation, is a pyramid, with so little available interior
space, not an exceeding peculiar conception? I would
suppose the rationale was that those who were to trans-
port the body to eternity would arrive from the sky, which
made it essential that the burial chamber should with-
stand the violence of such a momentous event. The
Egyptians practiced the transformation of death into
continuing life by placing vases of food of all categories
for the culinary palates of the dead.

There appears to have been a bad period in the 12–13th
millennium B.C., a period which provided the opportunity for the labour force on the pyramids to escape out of
Egypt. I do not have much belief in the existence of the
Hebrews before *Exodus*. What seems to have happened
was a rejection of the Egyptian pantheon by the labour
force, or a part of it, and possibly by a schism among the
Egyptians themselves. Rejection could not have been too
difficult, since by then the pantheon had become so weird

as to have excited the admiration of the most tortuous of African witch-doctors. In place of the dubious Egyptian pantheon there was a return to the dominance of a single god, Zeus in early times, Yahwey to the Hebrews, essentially the same idea. About whom the less said the better, an angry god, a god of vengeance, a god of vile temper. Wouldn't any sensible creature who had to cope with humans soon develop a vile temper?

A benign interval started about 1000 BC and lasted through classical times until the fifth and sixth centuries AD, passing thence through the Dark Ages back to a benign interval in modern times. The already attenuated ancient religions were essentially destroyed by the time of Thucydides, *circa* 420 BC. The ancient religions persisted thereafter more by inertia than conviction. Judaism resisted the usual tendency to pantheonism through the sustained ferocity of its religious leaders, only to be threatened eventually by the reformers of the Christian era in an unusual way. Instead of God being dark and vengeful, God was to be a kindly old father, otherwise the provisions of Judaism were to be maintained. Christianity was a view the Jews were right to reject because at the next bad period it would lead to complications, and to immense distortions from the views of its founder.

It has always been something of a puzzle as to why among what appears to have been a number of similar sects it should have been Christianity which survived. Possibly it was that for nearly forty years the sect continued by an oral tradition. After preaching to hundreds of small groups the story of Christ was shaped by the disciples to a form which secured optimum acceptance, whereas had it been written down immediately it would likely have had less appeal. And with preaching to ever wider audiences, and with four somewhat variable shots at a written form, the sect just about managed to maintain itself as an ongoing entity. St. Paul, the impresario for Christianity as for Christ. The Jews survived because they were a meta-historical people beyond the ancient Greeks, Egyptians, and Babylonians as a work force by virtue of the Decalogues.

The old religions had become too attenuated to survive the next bad period of *circa* AD500. Judaism was too particular to the Jews to secure widespread acceptance and Christianity gained rapid advance essentially by default, essentially because there was nothing else available. In a bad period a dash of strong medicine was needed however. God could not be a loving father unless the world was riddled by sundry devils, who became the cause of all disasters. Christianity became a defiance of reality, which actually aided its success. Instead of the threat from the skies being the cause of devastation, the sky was declared perfect and unchanging (the Moon excepted), a fiction aided by the circumstance that there were never any direct witnesses to what happened when a missile fell from the sky, for there were never any direct survivors, as there was with the explosion of Vesuvius in AD 79. Additionally too, one can suspect that such factual accounts as might have existed were ruthlessly suppressed over the centuries which followed the collapse of Rome.

The severity of the prohibition against changes in the sky is well-illustrated by the supernova of AD 1054.

Despite the supernova being brighter than Venus for weeks on end, there is no surviving European record of its occurrence. Over the centuries, hundreds of millions of Europeans must have noticed naked-eye spots on the Sun—without any effort I have seen them several times myself. Yet again there seem to have been no written accounts of their occurrence. Evidently then, Europe became gripped by a stultifying amnesia that was to prove a nearly impossible barrier to the development of science.

Victor Clube tells me that Isaac Newton was most reluctant to accept Halley's discovery of an Earth-crossing comet, because he saw immediately the possibility of impacts occurring, something he was intensely conditioned to avoid. It was only after Newton had decided comets evaporate into harmless gas and small particles that he was willing to accept Halley's contention. Just how deeply the desire went to attribute evil to what lay below ground rather than in the sky is shown by an interesting passage towards the end of Chapter 43 of Edward Gibbons *Decline and Fall of the Roman Empire*. After explaining on the authorities of Flamsteed, Cassini, Bernoulli, Newton and Halley that it was impossible for disasters to come from the sky, Gibbons wrote the following revealing but implausible passage. Implausible because earthquakes, while dangerous and deadly, hardly occur with the frequency or in the manner which Gibbon supposed:

". . . history will distinguish . . . periods in which calamitous events have been rare or frequent and will observe that this fever of the Earth raged with uncommon violence during the reign of Justinian (AD 527–565). Each year is marked by the repetition of earthquakes, of such duration that Constantinople has been shaken about forty days; of such extent that the shock has been communicated to the whole surface of the globe, or at least of the Roman Empire. An impulse or vibratory motion was felt, enormous chasms were opened up, huge and heavy bodies were discharged into the air, the sea alternately advanced and retreated beyond its ordinary bounds, and a mountain was torn from Libanus and cast into the waves . . . The stroke that agitates an ant-hill may crush the insect myriads in the dust . . . Two hundred and fifty thousand people are said to have perished . . . at Antioch."

After the early chapters of this immensely long work, I have to admit to finding Gibbon unreadable. The detail is so great, and the failure of the many threads to weave into a clear pattern so evident, as to give the impression of mere random noise, which is what would be expected of a once powerful empire breaking-up inescapably under the impact of missiles from the sky. The territory controlled by the Roman Empire was much greater than the several thousand square miles of destruction created by an individual impact. So one might think of a kind of chess board in which squares were knocked individually out of operation, with an attempt to fill-in again from surrounding squares after each such event, so producing a random ebb and flow of people and power. There have been diverse attempts at explaining the demise of the Roman Empire—wrong economic policies, poisoning from lead piping and the like—none of them plausible. The cause lies much more reasonably with missile impacts resulting in an incoherent toing and froing, just as Gibbon reads.

The new religion of the age was Islam. It appears no accident that Mohammed was born in AD 529, the same age as that of Justinian when the shock of something was "communicated to the whole surface of the globe . . ." It appears no accident either that Mohammed came out of the desert. Just as bombing raids in the Second World War did much more damage from fire than from the explosive energy they released, so it is likely that the heat released by missiles breaking up in the sky did more damage in Roman cities and in the forests of N. Europe than their explosive energy. The advantage of Muslims from the desert was that they were not surrounded by wood. The desert is not unstable against fire. And just as Christianity expanded into the sudden vacuum created by the demise of the Roman Empire, so did Islam, in a movement which still gains strength to this day, spurred by the eventual weakening of Christianity.

EMERGENCE INTO MEDIEVAL AND MODERN TIMES

The position of the scientifically minded in the better days of the Roman Empire was similar in many ways to the situation in the Soviet Union in modern times, encouragement for any idea of military importance and for little else. In a slave society improvements of convenience and in the production of goods of importance to the individual had a poor chance of attracting favourable attention. With the coming of the Dark Ages the situation was inverted, the emphasis of invention being focused down into what was relevant to individuals and to localised communities. Out of this inversion a far better state of affairs was presented to the inventively minded, as is apparent with the emergence of many discoveries into the more ordered society of medieval times. The windmill, the mechanical saw, forge with tilt hammer, wheelbarrow, window glass, the domestic chimney, candles and paved roads became widespread in the

12th century; spectacles, the wheeled plough, the ship's rudder, lock gates on canals, the grandfather clock and gunpowder in the 13th century.

The Christian Church emerged into medieval Europe with unfettered power over the minds of men. It was to engage in the nearly inevitable process of pantheon building. It added Christ to the loving Father, teetering over the centuries with adding Mary the mother of Christ. To the shadowy pantheon of angels it added a minor pantheon of saints and a major pantheon of devils. When Jeanne d'Arc answered charges against Devil 27 she was told the accusation was against Devil 42—there were actually 119 articles against the unfortunate Jeanne. By going along enthusiastically with saint creation, the Cornish and Bretons did best, reducing the process to the ridicule it deserved. We have St. Austell. Who was Austell? Who was St. Blazey? Then there were the saints Miniver, Mawgan and Mervyn. My favourite is St. Teath.

It was against this intellectual mess that science had to make progress, which it did in a considerable measure by sheer luck. The first major clash between science and the Church is that we associate with the heliocentric theory of Copernicus (1473–1543) who was born only forty-odd years after the trial of Jeanne d'Arc, which is to say into a world brimming with devils. The theory first germinated in the Renaissance interlude at the end of the 15th century, but with that easing of the intellectual climate soon passing, Copernicus, after refining his work *circa* 1525, did not seek to publish it. However, towards the end of his life he was visited by a young German who contrived to make a copy, the copy being eventually published in Wittenberg in 1542–43. Here was a slice of both irony and luck. Martin Luther had perhaps even less use for Copernicus than Copernicus' own Church, and yet it was Luther's Protestant breakaway from Rome which permitted the publication of de revolutionibus orbium coelestium and which therefore kept the heliocentric theory alive over the century or more which it took to establish itself beyond all point of recall.

Another stroke of luck was the bedroom farce of Henry VIII, taking place contemporaneously with Copernicus' later years. The decisive work of Johann Kepler in Protestant Germany at the beginning of the 17th century established the scientific position, forming the second act in the drama. The third act was the general acceptance in the mid-17th century in Protestant England, the general acceptance which formed the springboard for Newton's theory of gravitation in the 1680's. Before the die was at last cast, it took a century and a half from Copernicus to Newton, not a rapid affair. High in the credit list must go Anne Boleyn who started Henry's bedroom farce. In a just world Anne would surely receive posthumous honorary election to the world's prestigious scientific academics. For Henry, one can perhaps suggest posthumous election to the exclusive London clubs including White's and the Marylebone Cricket Club.

It is usually represented that after a millennium in the mental prison house of the early Christian Church, science at last broke free and was then able to forge ahead into modern times. But this is an illusion, for science only exchanged the older religious prison house for a new one of its own making. The situation was permitted only because Newton's explanation of the motions of the planets appeared to give a rational basis for what religious opinion wanted to believe in any case, namely that the Earth is unaffected from outside itself. Victor Clube's reference to Newton's worry over Earth-crossing cometary orbits indicates that Newton was himself highly sensitive on this point. Thus science was made to support a continuing amnesia over the Earth's past history, an amnesia which science has worked hard to maintain ever since, worked hard almost to the point of religious intensity. Indeed one might see the modern decline of the Christian Church as a consequence of science now doing its job more effectively than the Church is currently able to do.

In the wake of Newton's *Principia*, observatories were established throughout Europe. Occasionally they provided something useful—time-keeping and navigational aids at sea—but in the main astronomy prospered as a teller of interesting stories, and by no means as a study relevant to the march of human affairs. Court astronomers and their reflections in universities were like the musician Don Basilio in Mozart's *Marriage of Figaro*, very ready to retail tidbits, but careful to keep well out of the way whenever anything important happened.

Physics and chemistry were represented as sciences that could manage their affairs essentially without reference to anything outside the Earth, and for a long time this turned out to be true. Physics in particular moved far ahead of astronomy in utility value and in popular esteem. But from the mid-20th century onwards, physics went into something of a decline that must I think be interpreted as a consequence of amnesia. Physics has by now progressed as far as it can go without connecting itself to the universe in a fundamental way. Biology remains what it has always been, weak hypotheses allied to complex empiricism. These are the abiding consequences of shutting out the sky as a causative agent, as it was done a millennium and a half ago. Science has itself locked the door of its own cell, throwing away the keys through its own barred window, not a situation that calls for much celebration.

Clube and Napier point out that the bite is still there. The medieval monk Gervase of Canterbury recorded that according to five reliable witnesses on the evening of 25 June in the year AD 1178, the crescent Moon was seen to writhe like a wounded snake. The Moon, being an earthy kind of body, did not have to maintain in the medieval mind the same changeless inviolability as the stars. This observation of 25 June 1178 was due to dust particles thrown from the lunar surface up into the sunlight by a major impact, an impact considerably larger than a Tunguska event. The likely crater produced by the impact has been identified in recent years, and the small vibrations of the Moon which the impact caused, and which will die away in the medium-term future, have actually been detected. Had such an event occurred on the Earth, human survival over an area of hundreds of thousands of square miles would have been problematical.

This event shows that it is now time for the human ostrich to get its head out of the sand. Although it seems that the dissolution of the giant comet of Clube and Napier may be approaching its end, there is no guarantee that the Earth will not experience a further major episode of Tunguska-like events. Reckoning free periods as lasting one to two millennia, and reckoning the last one at AD 500, the next episode might well be not more than a century or two ahead. On this basis let us see by way of conclusion what has to be done. The first step is to compile a catalogue of all objects of appreciable size in Earth-crossing orbits. For this a space telescope is needed. But not as large or as expensive as the Hubble Telescope. One with an aperture of a metre should be adequate, at any rate initially. It could be seen as curious that society would seek to investigate distant galaxies while at the same time ignoring all possibility of serious impacts with the Earth, surely a clear example of amnesia in action. Even if all the above is discounted, the compiling of a catalogue of potential dangers is an important thing to do, and the circumstance that it is not being done can be seen essentially as a proof that what was said above is correct. Only blind amnesia can explain it. The second step is to refine the observations sufficiently for precise orbits to be calculated and for serious threats to be identified at the earliest possible stage. The ultimate third step would be to deflect those for which collision with the Earth may be imminent, a process that would need hitting an object with a mass of some tens of tons of material at a high speed. When this third stage is reached, mankind can at last wake up from the strange nightmare of the past.

REFERENCES

The Cosmic Winter by Victor Clube and Bill Napier, Blackwell, Oxford, 1990.

Our Universes, Sir Denys Wilkinson, Columbia University Press, New York, 1991.

DISCUSSION

Dr. Anshen: I have been impressed again and again and again by cosmologists, both Big Bang and Steady State, that the universe knows in advance what step it has to take before it takes it. My question then is: since the implication is that the universe is cognitive, since knowing is a cognitive term, and cognition implies consciousness, and consciousness implies will, purpose, determination, decision, does the universe think? And, though it may not be answered in our present state of information and knowledge, I still have faith in the reality of possibility that one day, prayerfully, this question may be answered.

Professor Freeman J. Dyson: Now I have a list of about seven people who have volunteered or been volunteered to discuss this talk. And I don't know whether I should call on you each in term or whether you would just spontaneously rise and go to the microphones. Which would you like to do? I myself did not prepare a speech. I have some comments to make if the discussion flags, but I don't think this is very likely.

Professor Paul O. Kristeller: I'd like to begin with the section at the end of the talk, which dealt with the origin of religions. I don't know much about the subject, but I only want to comment that it seems to me a strange chronology that dates the Homeric religion back to the time before 4,000, almost a millenium and a half before the old Egyptian religion. That seems to me a strange chronology, although I am not a historian of religion, and therefore cannot document what I say.

I am more concerned about the main issue, the question of the Big Bang and its alternative that was not labeled today, but I understand is called Steady State. Am I right? And I must say I'm a layman and do not know anything about cosmology, and I wouldn't have ventured to talk in this discussion unless I was encouraged when I voiced some questions.

First of all, the observation of the Big Bang seemed to me strange. Why should, in an infinite and uncontrollable universe, the universal system as we know it arise suddenly? And I cannot help feeling that the great applause which this theory found among many people has something to do with the spread of fundamentalism. I mean people love to think that very intricate cosmology would confirm what many people nowadays believe, that the account of creation in the Bible is basically right. And so there is a willingness to believe this. I personally am not a fundamentalist and I would say that I felt a bit of diffidence when I heard this theory discussed and applauded from circles both Jewish and Christian, which somehow fits their preconceptions regardless of the evidence.

On the other hand, I find the alternative, the so-called Steady State, much more plausible because my interest is in Greek philosophy, and I find that it is more in agreement with certain forms of Greek philosophical speculation. Not with Plato, because Plato's *Timaeus*—myth or not—is reconcilable with creation. Not with Aristotle, because he assumes that there is only a single cosmos, which is eternal. In a sense it comes closer to Aristotle than to Plato.

But it comes closest to something that is not widely understood or known, namely, to the atomistic theory, and to certain views voiced by Democritus, by Epicurus and Lucretius, and in more modern times by Gassendi and by Giordano Bruno, who cite these authorities. They assume that there is an infinite universe, and within this infinite universe there are smaller worlds that come and go. And I find that the alternative hinted at by Sir Fred Hoyle comes closer to this. And I find it, for that reason, more plausible, because I am more interested in Greek philosophy than in various forms of contemporary religion. And I hope that Sir Hoyle may not find this completely unacceptable.

Professor John Wheeler: To speak against "closed-box" thinking is more appropriate for Fred Hoyle than anybody else I can name because he has done so much to make clear the tie between one thing and another. Of all the developments which occupy an honorable place in the story of science, nothing is more wonderful than what he and William Fowler have done to explain how the elements were created. "The still warm ashes of creation" is the lovely phrase that Victor Weisskoff coined for radioactivity, which is the record of elements slowly decaying.

I can recall at the time I was a visitor to the National Laboratories on the question of radioactivity: how much was escaping and all the methods that were being adopted to check up on contaminations. And finally, one colleague at Los Alamos had developed a tank filled with what looked like water but was actually water with an ingredient in it that gave the water the right to be called scintillation fluid. Any radioactive particle passing into this fluid produced light, which could be picked up by counters placed all around the box. One member of the laboratory after another was immersed in this, like baptism, and some odd things were found. The men showed more radioactivity than the women. Was this because they were working more often with radioactive materials? Certainly not. And finally somebody realized what the reason was. Potassium is one of "the still warm ashes of creation." Potassium has a natural radioactivity and potassium accumulates in muscle. Perhaps there were one or two women athletes who could have changed the record.

But this reach across time and space is nowhere more impressive, of course, than in cosmology, and in this question about the Big Bang and the question of what triggered it off. I confess that I escape from that question myself by saying the Big Bang was a time before which there was no time, as a "Big Crunch," if there is to be one, by the same token, is a moment after which there is no time.

I could recall Einstein confessing his turning away from Big Bang cosmology when he first hit on it in 1915. He had applied his new general relativity theory of gravitation to the motion of light passing the sun, the escape of radiation from the sun, and the motion of Mercury around the sun. Then he turned to cosmology and he found, to his distress, that there was no place for an ever-persistent universe. How come that he took that as a death blow to that picture? He himself has explained in more than one place that his greatest hero was Spinoza. And Spinoza was excommunicated from the Amsterdam Synagogue in the 1600s for denying the Biblical account of creation. And how come? Because, where would the clock set, Spinoza felt, in all that nothingness, before anything began, to tell it when to start. Self-contradictory theory.

So Fred Hoyle incites us to connect the near and the far. And if archaeology is the art of making trenches and digging up what one comes to and interpreting the relation of one thing to another, then one could say that astrophysics is the greatest of trenches. We are digging a trench through the records of the past all the way to the Big Bang.

But connecting life with the physical universe brings up a whole range of questions that I think we were right not to get into tonight. The question, if the universe is necessary to the creation of life, could it be that life is necessary to the creation of the universe? Do acts of observership, in the quantum sense, have anything to do with bringing about that which appears before us. Nothing is more mysterious in the subject of quantum mechanics than the role of the observer in the scheme of things.

Some of my colleagues take very seriously the concept of the anthropic principle, the idea that one should visualize a great collection of universes, most of which have properties which will not permit life, but now and again one comes upon a rare one which permits life and in it the physical constants are so tuned that this is possible. But this picture really hardly saves the day because it replaces the mystery of where does the universe come from with a still bigger mystery of some super-machine which stamps out universes of various properties. Where does that super-machine come from?

I hope that I can just simply say here at the end that the reading of Darwin is always an inspiration. And one recalls from reading Darwin what a big place he gives to the existence of islands of development on the surface of the earth. The conditions of temperature and water, separated perhaps one from another by great regions of ice. This existence of regions of development, independent of one another, between which selection can operate and give favored place to those worthy accidents of evolution, make the living system compatible with living conditions, reminds one of what we are doing here, talking about a range of ideas coming from many different fields between which we could look at which are the ones which fit. And we can all thank our lucky stars that there are such things as great monasteries, great centers of reflection, centers of light and learning, which are animated by different outlooks so that in them too we can have this evolutionary history that has held for life happening in the life of the mind.

So I am truly grateful to Fred for his inspiration.

Professor James Schwartz: I've been asked as a neuroscientist to comment on Sir Fred's presentation. And, before I start, I'd like to say that I have nothing really against religion that doesn't contradict art history. The idea that the Sistine Chapel is pointed to the Last Judgement, I think is questionable from a neuroscientist's point of view since the Last Judgement was painted many, many years after the Creation and probably reflects Michelangelo's disappointment, depression with his life, and the life of his times.

I am in no position actually to sense how significant was the effect of comets on history. Sir Fred has presented a plausible correlation of bombardments by extraterrestrial bodies with crucial turning points in human affairs. However significant historically and prehistorically, Sir Fred's lecture can surely be taken as a parable illustrating the impact of the rest of the universe on human life and consciousness, a parable warning us against what he has called "closed-box" thinking. And this may be particularly pertinent to my field, neuroscience.

I would not have anticipated that astronomers and neuroscientists would have had very much to say to each other when I was an undergraduate in the 1950s and even as recently as a decade ago. To us, cosmologists sat on mountain tops far from urban environments looking away from life, whereas we biologists worked in our laboratories looking into nerve cells. While they could only have limited contact with their experimental material, we could examine the nervous system of many creatures, from mollusks to man. Our material was right there. We could touch it, tame it, stick microelectrodes in it, extract it, and sometimes even synthesize parts of it in a test tube. This hands-on approach with our experimental material stems in large part from a long biomedical tradition.

For the past two centuries, the mainstream approach to brain and behavior has been biomedical. Analysis of the mind was usurped from philosophers, first by nineteenth-century neurologists, then by psychiatrists and behavioral psychologists, and now by neuropharmacologists and by cell and molecular biologists.

A few neuroscientists at the fringe were also aware of cybernetics, information theory, and artificial intelligence as they developed out of engineering, experimental physics, and mathematics. But it is only since the mid-1980s that neuroscience has become a blend of "closed-box" biology based on reductionist molecular techniques and a "closed-box" epistemology based on communications and information processing. And now, all of a sudden, cosmology bombards the world of neuroscience.

One aspect of Sir Fred's parable seems particularly pertinent and that is that some extraterrestrial events carry important information. Thus bombardments by comets are not only instances of catastrophic events to which humans have had to react passively, but they also carry information. They are not only brute facts, but also revelations. To illustrate, the bright flash of light from a distant bombardment in Siberia that Miss Stevens saw at dawn on the first of July 1908 was rather meaningless. But the bombardments that occurred around 6,000 B.C. are postulated to have suggested the idea of smelting and therefore to have introduced the Bronze Age.

Twenty-six years ago, Sir Fred was involved in the analysis of another aspect of extraterrestrial information transfer. The transfer of astronomical information as reflected in the standing stones of Scotland and Western Europe and of Stonehenge, that great prehistoric observatory, or perhaps cathedral in Wiltshire. Even though this information was received without physical catastrophe, the idea of time, the years, the seasons, months, days and nights surely is also a fine example of extraterrestrial information transfer.

From a neuroscientist's point of view, however, what is important is the methodological assumptions that Sir Fred made in two interesting papers that appeared in 1966 that were designed to decide whether Stonehenge was used for measuring alignments of astronomical bodies in the second millenium B.C. He asked, "How would *we* do it." And he answered, "an excellent procedure for *us* to follow would be to build a structure of the pattern of Stonehenge."

Now he made two key assumptions here. First, that the brains of humans in the second millenium were quite like ours. And two, that extraterrestrial information or, for that matter, any information about nature would not be received without those brains. The first assumption is commonplace evolutionary reasoning, totally expected since our species, homo sapiens, evolved with a modern brain about 40,000 years ago.

The second assumption is cryptically revolutionary because it borders on a statement of what I believe cosmologists call the anthropic principle. Since there are an overwhelming and enormously threatening number of distinguished cosmologists and physicists in this auditorium, I wouldn't dare to assess how significant the impact of cosmology will be on neuroscience. I feel somewhat safer to quote Roger Penrose, a cosmologist who is *not* present tonight. Penrose asked, "How important is consciousness to the universe as a whole? Could a universe exist without any conscious inhabitants whatever? Are the laws of physics specially designed in order to allow the existence of conscious life? Is there something special about our particular location in the universe, either in space or time?"

Clearly these questions, if meaningful, bear directly on neuroscience. At present, I wonder whether the answers could arise from modern cell and molecular biology, on one hand, or from computer modeling of neuro-networks.

Professor Roger Shinn: My name is Roger Shinn and my scholarly discipline is Christian social ethics. I appreciate the invitation to respond to Sir Fred, who, once again, has shown us his fertility of mind and his ability to bring fresh insights to any subject.

I'll center my comments on his discussion of religion. Here he has limited his evidence to a rather small part of the planet, neglecting most of Asia, including the religions of the *Rig Veda*, the *Upanishads*, the *Mahabharata*, including the *Bhagavad Gita*, the work of Confucius, Lao-tse, and so on. And he has limited his view of religion in the last five thousand years or so, omitting the origins of religion, which were many centuries earlier.

What do we mean by religion? Santayana called religion the response to the mystery and pathos of existence, to which I would add, the ecstasy and the tragedy. Julian Huxley described it as "an agency for expressing, affirming, and struggling with [human] destiny in mingled awe and adoration." And to that I would add penitence and aspiration. The chief expressions of religion are worship, both cultic and mystical, ethical commitment, and intellectual doctrine. It takes many forms; animism, totemism, polytheism, henotheism, pantheism, monotheism, naturalism, humanism, usually nationalistic but sometimes universal.

And its origins are, as far as we can tell, about as old as the emergence of authentically human life on the planet. Dobzhansky related it to the rise of self-awareness and death-awareness, and he found evidence of it in the burial customs of Neanderthal man almost 200,000 years ago.

Now if you look at more recent times, Karl Jaspers found a great leap in human history in what he called "the axial period," from about 800 to about 500 B.C.E. This was the era of the Chinese sages, of the Upanishads and the Buddha, the Hebrew prophets, the Greek tragedians—and Plato just barely fits in. Interestingly, that does not fit any of Sir Fred's critical periods at 1,600-year intervals, and it suggests a very different conceptualization of religious origins in history.

Religion comes in great variety. It is creative and destructive. It inspires war and peace, fanaticism and forgiveness. The evaluation of it requires discriminate judgements. The problem is that the criteria for judgement are themselves religious. Religious thought, like most human thought, rarely escapes an element of circular reasoning.

To turn to Biblical faith, which I know best, I must disagree with Sir Fred's stark contrast between the Hebrew Bible and the character of Jesus. He sees accurately the Jahweh of Hosts, the Lord mighty in battle. He misses the God who is slow to anger and plenteous in mercy. It was the Hebrew prophets who insisted that the God who judges the sins of those nations out there, also judges the sins of Israel, that the God who saves Israel also saves the nations, that the God who ordains government on earth also condemns kings and the powerful who oppress the common people. Through those prophets, fallible and unsophisticated in many ways, the world has been given a glimpse of a justice and a mercy encompassing all people.

We can discuss these issues for a long, long time. I half-regret that neither Sir Fred nor I will be available to discuss them in the year 2100, when the next strike of giant comet remnants may test the judgements of both of us.

Professor Milton Gatch: When I was asked to be a respondent to Sir Fred's lecture my first reaction was that I would be utterly out of my water this evening and I think that was right in this setting. What, after all, can a student of religion in the Middle Ages say about great issues of modern cosmology, especially as framed by a cosmologist who has so dim a view of both religion and the Middle Ages.

It did occur to me that there is a certain irony in the fact that cosmology has become the purview of physics and astronomy. My desk dictionary still gives the definition of cosmology as a philosophical subject priority over its definition as a branch of astrophysics. Even so it does not allude to cosmology as a branch of theology. Yet the creation of the universe has, not only because of the leading of the creation myth in Genesis, always been a subject of Christian theology. The great subject of the earliest Christian theologians, indeed, was theoretical or philosophical cosmology. They tried to explain their faith in a God who entered the realm of human history and human affairs—their Hebrew heritage as it were—in a philosophical and religious milieu in which God was often conceived as utterly removed from time, space, and the physical world—their Hellenistic heritage.

The end of the universe as we know it has likewise been a major subject of theological cosmology, albeit a much maligned one. It is interesting to learn that the end of the universe is now a subject of interest to astrophysicists. We do not often remember in our time that in the program of Michelangelo for the Sistine Chapel in the Vatican Palace, although the creation begins the historical panels of the ceilings—which one must contort oneself to see—it is the end of history that directly confronts the person in the Chapel who turns her or his attention to the altar and the wall behind it. And that is where our attention is intended primarily to dwell.

DISCUSSION

If the Greeks had a picture of the universe as eternal, stable, based on unchanging conditions and truth from which we have fallen away into a debased and physical world, the Christians had a picture of the universe as a created and purposeful system. These two pictures of the cosmos have stood in tension in Western thought and that tension persists in the thought of the modern secular scientific cosmologists who view the universe as a Platonic steady state, and those who think of it as created *ex nihilo* in a Big Bang.

It was something of a disappointment to me to discover in Sir Fred's paper a prejudice against the Christian tradition as an intellectual tradition, and perhaps against Christianity, in particular, amongst the world religions. About that I want to say only here that I hope that he might reconsider the matter. Many professed Christians and many of the institutions created by that religion have been morally and intellectually limited, even obtuse, just as scientists too—as Sir Fred justly says—have also been intellectually limited. Michelangelo arose in the Christian intellectual tradition and continued it as I have already said.

As to Sir Fred's major thesis that the central moments of human history, moments that have been formative for religions—or at least of religions influential in our Western experience—that these central moments have coincided with the periodic impact upon the earth of fragments from the breakup of comets, I hardly know what to say. The theory is fascinating. I wish somewhat as our lecturer wishes that scientists did not so often approach the universe as a "closed box," that the examples of the influence of those cosmic events were not so largely limited to the Mediterranean world, for the effect surely would be on the whole earth.

And I also wish that there was time, among many other things, to talk about what is meant by "bad periods of history" that generated religions. I hail our lecturer above all for making us think about the future, by drawing our attention to a cosmic event just over a century off. And I could wish we might ask what that portended event, if we may accept it hypothetically at least, should mean about the way we live.

Professor Philip Solomon: I was glad that Dr. Wheeler brought up Fred Hoyle's contributions to the origin of the elements because we know that is one of the most successful theories in astrophysics. And, in that sense, Sir Fred has already connected the life of the stars with the life on earth because all of the elements that make up life, except for hydrogen and helium and a few others— but, for example, carbon, nitrogen, and oxygen—were made inside the stars. And we wouldn't be here tonight except for that event or events inside stars.

Now, what Sir Fred is telling us tonight is that he wants us to consider the possibility that not just the stars but the comets have affected life on earth and, in particular, have affected the recent history and prehistory of the earth, an idea actually almost as radical as his correct idea that the elements were formed in stars.

Now, I am certainly not an expert on any of the mythology or recent history, but it seems to me that the key part of the idea presented tonight is that the recent ice age was terminated by the impact of cometary debris onto the surface of the earth and that would require something ·like the giant comet he described. And it's a tempting idea because there is no question that if a large object fell into the oceans and heated the ocean, the rapid evaporation of the oceans would indeed increase the temperature of the earth very rapidly. It would be a super greenhouse effect, something which we are reading about in the newspaper everyday lately, and this would make the current greenhouse menace seem rather minor and that could reverse the ice age.

So the real question comes down to, specifically, is there a giant comet with a period of 1,600 years. That is really what, I think, his specific talk was about. I don't know the answer to that, but like most of Fred's predictions it's going to be testable. It will be testable, probably, certainly in the next fifty to 100 years for sure. Because if this comet exists—I may have done this wrong, Fred, I'm not sure—but it should be somewhere between ten, twenty, or thirty astronomical units out, right about now. And sometime within the next fifty years we should be able to see it. So, if you hang on for the next fifty years, we will find out whether Sir Fred was correct tonight.

Professor Norman Newell: I have been asked to give a geologist's reactions to Sir Fred's stimulating remarks. To start with, I should point out that earth scientists share with the astronomers the awareness that the earth is not isolated in space. It is after all made of nebular materials. It is warmed by the sun, visited frequently by meteorites, and alternations of ice and greenhouse agents. The earth is subject to irregularities in its trip around the sun as well as movements within the solid earth.

The fossil record tells much about the history of the earth. The oldest fossils are all marine microorganisms, some 3.5 billion years old. The first many-celled plants and animals did not appear until almost 3 billion years later, after completion of 86 percent of all of life's history. The human species did not emerge until the last fraction of the last one percent of the time since the world was born, 4.5 billion years earlier. This was an uncertain and probably unique process. Why did it take so long? Ask yourself that. The development of life was complex and uncertain. Even before the appearance of many-celled organisms 600 million years ago, there were fluctuations in the abundance of life. The episodic character of the record is even more pronounced in the younger strata. Evolutionary diversification was interrupted over and over again by climatic oscillations and the mass extinctions of major groups. Two explanations for the extinctions are often cited.

Firstly, that the earth collided with large objects, which is Sir Fred's preference. The extinction of the dinosaurs and contemporary animals at the end of the Cretaceous period is used as an example of the Alvarez impact theory, first published in 1980. Sir Fred stresses comets, but comets are relatively rare. They are outnumbered by meteorites by several orders of magnitude. Most extinction events are not known to be closely related in time with either ice ages or impact craters.

The second explanation, which I prefer, speculates that extinctions resulted from complex changes in world environments, including those in the interior of the earth. Glacial cycles, in the conventional explanations, are the product of the earth's motions around the sun. Their orbit is elliptical, causing cyclic alternations of the amount of sunlight received. Furthermore, the earth's spin axis is tilted and the tilt itself slowly rotates. These and other anomalies impress small cycles upon larger cycles that have been well studied by astronomers.

Geologists have a test of this. They find that precisely the same complex patterns are preserved in the oceanic sediments of the past. This is known as the Malenkovich theory of glaciation. It is also thought by geologists to be one explanation of the alternate warming and cooling. It becomes evident that comets are not needed for this phenomenon.

If I may conclude. Sir Fred has touched on the relation between astronomy and theology. I'll leave that for the theologians to discuss, but in my view science and religion seem to be converging. Nature is orderly, in which every effect has an antecedent cause. The physical universe is managed by deterministic laws, modulated by quantum uncertainty. And all life is designed on the same two macro-molecules of carbon isotope and a single genetic code. The Big Bang theory has brought wide attention to the origin of the universe and creation. But let us ask, how did the chemical elements, energy, and the natural laws and forces of physics originate. The old problem of a first cause has now become a major concern for scientists as it always has been for the theologians.

CONCLUSION

Sir Fred Hoyle: The issue of whether the universe is purposive is an ultimate question that is at the back of everybody's mind. And John Wheeler has touched on this question when he mentioned the anthropic principle and the greatest mysteries that one has in quantum mechanics with the role of the observer. And Dr. Anshen has now just raised exactly the same question as to whether the universe is a product of thought. And I have to say that that is also my personal opinion, but I can't, back it up by too much of precise argument. There are very many aspects of the universe where you have either to say there have been monstrous coincidences, which there might have been, or, alternatively, there is a purposive scenario to which the universe conforms.

I perhaps would just like to take the opportunity of having the final few words to draw attention to the last item in my table, that for the year 2100 to which Phil

Solomon has referred, and perhaps add a word about that. Because the question that one has to ask is whether there is any way, if this story has an element of truth in it, that we can respond actively to the threat that will occur around the year 2100 A.D. Phil Solomon has said that the comet, if it exists, is somewhere out beyond the orbit of Neptune at the moment. And, if you calculate how bright it would be, then we couldn't see it yet, and one would very much like, as the years go by, to look and see whether there is anything there, whether it is coming in.

If there is, what can we do about it? Well, it's very interesting that the things we can do about it are just in fact the things our society is doing technically. And you could say that the most striking success of the program, was the achievement of the Voyager spacecraft, that is, the two Voyager missions, which as you may recall went out progressively to the various outer planets and ultimately out of the solar system. The techniques that were used on that marvelous success are just the kind of techniques, which, in their beginning, would enable us to take an active defense role. We have to know where the bits of the comets are. We have to record them. We have to know what their orbits are. And this involves a tremendous amount of high-speed tracking by telescopes, computer work, and ultimately the response has to come not from Star Wars but from very far-reaching developments of that concept.

You can't put an object out from the earth that is going to hit a dangerous missile and knock it off course all in one go. What you have to do is to put a missile out from the earth that hits an intermediate object, or perhaps several intermediate objects, like in a game of billiards where the balls progressively hit each other. You start by deflecting a smaller object and that hits a larger object, which ultimately hits the missile that you want to deflect.

Now when I look at the time scale that is involved and relate it to technology, I'm somewhat amazed that the time scale is just about right. We have about a century to go and if one postulates that things go on pretty well as they have been going on, I think we should be able to, by the year 2100, take an active role in preventing further disasters of the type that I've been mentioning.

It doesn't seem to me by any means hopeless, and that was lying, as it were, behind the reason I chose this subject. I'm not saying it's right. We've heard some objections. It may quite well be wrong. But the whole matter is serious enough for it to be aired because preparations, if it is correct, have to be taken early. And I think they can be taken and the case is by no means one to dispair over.

Professor Freeman Dyson: Well thank you very much, Sir Fred, for this delightfully upbeat ending, which to me was quite unexpected. Thank you all for your coming here and for the contributions you have made, and most of all thanks to Dr. Anshen for inviting us all.

BIOGRAPHICAL NOTES

RUTH NANDA ANSHEN, PH.D., Fellow of the Royal Society of Arts of London, founded, plans, and edits several distinguished series of books, including World Perspectives, Religious Perspectives, Credo Perspectives, Perspectives in Humanism, the Science of Culture Series, the Tree of Life Series, and Convergence. She has exerted remarkable influence through her worldwide lectures, her writings, her ability to attract a most important group of contributors to these series, underlying the unitary principle of all reality, and particularly through her close association with many of the great scientists and thinkers of this century, from Whitehead, Einstein, Bohr, and Heisenberg to Rabi, Tillich, Chomsky, and Wheeler. Dr. Anshen's book *Anatomy of Evil*, a study in the phenomenology of evil, demonstrates the interrelationship between good and evil. She is also the author of *Biography of an Idea* and the recent volume *Morals Equals Manners*.

Dr. Anshen is a member of the American Philosophical Association, the History of Science Society, the International Philosophical Society, and the Metaphysical Society of America.

Speaker   Sir Fred Hoyle

FRED HOYLE, known the world over for his leadership in the field of astrophysics, was educated at Emmanuel College, Cambridge, from which he graduated with top honors in mathematics. After serving with the British Admiralty during World War II, he returned to St. John's College, Cambridge, where he was a Fellow from 1939 to 1972. For him this was a period marked by extraordinary contributions in astrophysics, including the development of the Steady State Theory with Hermann Bondi and Thomas Gold and work on the formation of heavy elements in stars. He has held numerous other academic positions, including University Lecturer in Mathematics, Cambridge, 1845–58; Plumian Professor of Astronomy and Experimental Philosophy, Cambridge, 1958–72; Director, Institute of Theoretical Astronomy, Cambridge, 1967–73; Professor of Astronomy, Royal Institute of Great Britain, 1969–72; Staff Member, Mount Wilson and Palomar Observatories, 1957–62; Visiting Professor of Astronomy, California Institute of Technology, 1953–56; and Andrew D. White Professor at Large, Cornell University, 1972–68.

Sir Fred was named Fellow of the Royal Society in 1957 and an Honorary Fellow of St. John's College, Cambridge, in 1973. He received the Gold Medal of the

Royal Astronomical Society, 1968; the Kalinga Prize, United Nations, 1968; the Bruce Gold Medal, Astronomical Society of the Pacific, 1970; and the Royal Medal, Royal Society, 1974. He was knighted in 1972. Sir Fred is the author of numerous publications in astronomy, astrophysics, and cosmology, including *Man in the Universe* (1966), *Diseases From Space* (1979, with N.C. Wickramasinghe), and *The Intelligent Universe* (1983), as well as many novels and stories.

Discussion Leader   Freeman J. Dyson, Professor of Physics, Institute for Advanced Study

FREEMAN DYSON was educated at Winchester College and at Cambridge University, from which he received his degree in mathematics in 1945. He went on to become a Fellow of Trinity College, Cambridge, then studied at Cornell University under a Commonwealth Fellowship and served as Research Fellow at the University of Birmingham. In 1951 he became Professor of Physics at Cornell University, and two years later he was appointed Professor of Physics at the Institute for Advanced Study, Princeton, where he remains today. He has held visiting professorships at Yeshiva University and the Max-Planck-Institute for Physics and Astrophysics in Munich, and has consulted extensively in various branches of government, in particular the weapons laboratories, the Space Agency, the Disarmament Agency, and the Defense Department.

Professor Dyson's awards and honors include membership in the Royal Society (1952) and the U.S. Academy of

Sciences (1964), the Danny Heineman Prize of the American Institute of Physics, the Lorentz Medal of the Royal Netherlands Academy, the Hughes Medal of the Royal Society, the Max Planck Medal of the German Physical Society, the J. Robert Oppenheimer Memorial Prize from the Center for Theoretical Studies in Miami, and the Harvey Prize of the Technion, Haifa, Israel.

His publications include *Disturbing the Universe* (1979), *Weapons and Hope* (1984, which that year won the National Books Critics Award for Non-Fiction), *Origins of Life* (1986), and *Infinite in All Directions* (1988).

Discussants
Professor Paul Oscar Kristeller:
Woodbridge Professor Emeritus of
Philosophy, Columbia University

Professor John Archibald Wheeler,
Joseph Henry Professor of Physics Emeritus,
Princeton University

Dr. James H. Schwartz: Scientist and
Scholar in Neuro-Biology, College of
Physicians and Surgeons, Columbia University
Presbyterian Center.

Professor Roger Shinn: Professor of
Christian Theology, Union Theological
Seminary, New York City.

Professor Milton Gatch:
Professor of Theology and Director of the
Burke Library, Union Theological Serminary,
New York City

Professor Philip Solomon: Professor of
Astronomy, State University of New York
at Stony Brook, Long Island, New York.

Norman Newell: Professor of Geology, Paeleontology,
and Ecology at the American Museum
of Natural History in New York City,
New York.

COLOPHON

The text is set in Melior, a typeface designed by
Hermann Zapf in 1952. The type is composed by
Books International, Deatsville, Alabama. The
book is printed on acid free 60# Glatfelter offset
B-16 Antique text paper.

This book is the textual part of a lecture series
held at The Frick Collection in New York conceived and edited by Ruth Nanda Anshen.